# THE CHANGING FACE OF
# THAILAND

## Text by TERRY CLAYTON

HODDER
Wayland

an imprint of Hodder Children's Books

© 2004 White-Thomson Publishing Ltd

Produced for Hodder Wayland by
White-Thomson Publishing Ltd
2/3 St Andrew's Place
Lewes BN7 1UP

Editor: Elaine Fuoco-Lang
Designer: Clare Nicholas
Concept Design: Chris Halls, Mind's Eye Design
Consultant: Dr Ian Elgie

First published in Great Britain in 2004 by Hodder Wayland, an imprint of
Hodder Children's Books.

British Library Cataloguing in Publication Data
Clayton, Terry
   The Changing Face of Thailand
   1. Human geography - Thailand - Juvenile literature
   2. Thailand - history - 1945 - Juvenile literature
   I. Title  II. Thailand
   959.3'04

ISBN 0 7502 4270 1

Printed in Hong Kong

Hodder Children's Books
A division of Hodder Headline Limited
338 Euston Road, London NW1 3BH

**Acknowledgements**
The publishers would like to thank
the following for their contributions
to this book: Rob Bowden – statistics
research; Peter Bull – map illustration;
Nick Hawken – statistics panel
illustration.

# Contents

# 1 Samut Prakan

**Barometer of change**

Thailand is divided up into 76 provinces. The capital city of each province has the same name as the province. Samut Prakan is a small province bordering Bangkok Metropolitan Area on the north and west. Samut Prakan province has seen many changes since it was founded in 1620. But it has changed the most rapidly in the last twenty years.

In the 1980s Samut Prakan was a sleepy fishing port. Families from Bangkok would visit Samut Prakan at the weekends to enjoy the relaxing environment. They would explore old forts and eat the delicious local seafood.

Today Samut Prakan is at the heart of great change. The province has become the most industrialized in Thailand. There are over 5,000 factories in Samut Prakan, more than any other province in Thailand. The population of the city of Samut Prakan increased by 50 per cent in the ten years between 1990 and 2000 because so many people from other provinces came to work in the factories. Like other growing cities in Thailand, Samut Prakan has problems with solid waste management, water quality and traffic.

▲ *An ancient Buddhist* chedi *can be seen just beyond a busy junction in central Samut Prakan.*

The people of Samut Prakan want to balance growth in manufacturing and tourism with quality of life and a good environment around their city. To help achieve this, the Thai government plans to build a main wastewater treatment plant in Samut Prakan province. Factory owners and tourism operators are being encouraged to use green technologies to conserve resources and remove polluting chemicals from the water they use before it goes back into nearby rivers and lakes.

In the second half of the 20th century, Thailand built a strong social and economic foundation and will continue to be one of the more stable and prosperous states in South-east Asia in the twenty-first century.

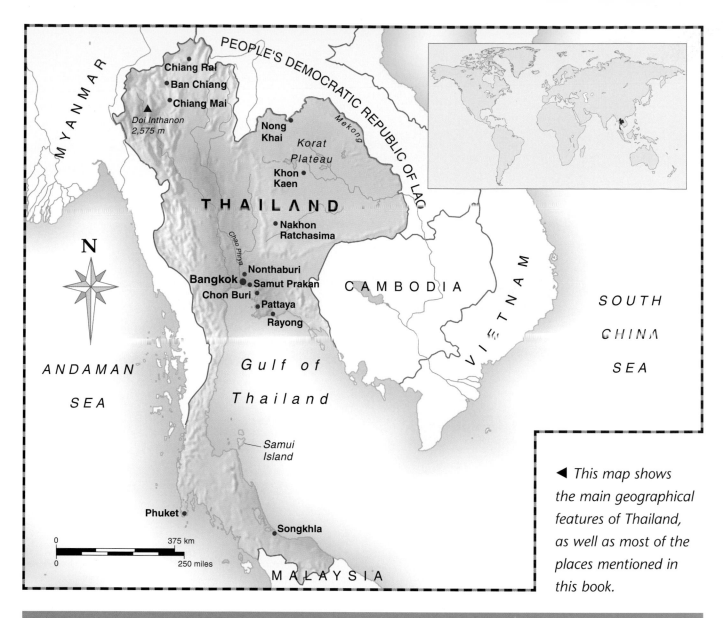

◄ *This map shows the main geographical features of Thailand, as well as most of the places mentioned in this book.*

## THAILAND: KEY FACTS

**Area:** 513,115 sq km

**Population:** 64 million

**Population density:** 125 people per sq km

**Capital city:** Bangkok (7.2 million)

**Other main cities:** Nonthaburi, Nakhon Ratchasima, Chon Buri, Chiang Mai

**Highest mountain:** Doi Inthanon (2,575 m)

**Longest river:** Chao Phraya (365 km)

**Main language:** Thai

**Major religions:** Buddhism (94 per cent), Islam (4 per cent), Christianity (1 per cent), other (1 per cent)

**Currency:** Thai baht (1 baht = 100 satang)

# Past Times

**From ancient kingdom to modern democracy**

People have been living in the area now known as Thailand for over 5,000 years. Some archaeologists consider the ancient village of Ban Chiang in north-eastern Thailand to be one of the oldest human settlements in South-east Asia.

Thailand used to be called the Kingdom of Siam until 1949 when the government officially changed the name to Thailand as part of a campaign to make the country more modern.

The first Siamese kingdom was in Sukothai more than 700 years ago. 'Sukothai' means 'dawn of happiness' and the 120 years of the Sukothai period are called the Golden Age of Thai history. King Ramkhamhaeng was one of the great kings of this period. He encouraged art, literature and Buddhism and he invented the Thai script.

▼ *Wat Phra Kaeo is part of the Grand Palace complex in Bangkok and is a dramatic example of Thai temple architecture.*

▲ *The democracy monument in central Bangkok symbolizes Thailand's commitment to an open society.*

## Modern Thailand

In 1932 Thailand became a constitutional monarchy like the United Kingdom. At various times between 1932 and 1992, military leaders succeeded in taking control of the government. In the 1950s, Thai governments started building a national road system, introduced manufacturing and started growing cash crops for export. By the mid 1980s, Thailand was one of the fastest-growing economies in the world. Since the fall of the last military government in 1992, Thailand has become a more open and democratic society.

▶ *Characters from a scene in a traditional Thai play, which is as popular today as in the past.*

# IN THEIR OWN WORDS

'My name is Chamras Bawornsiwamon. I am a teacher at Sriwittiya Paknam School in Samut Prakan. This is our computer lab. When I started teaching over 40 years ago, the parents of most students in Samut Prakan were farmers or fishermen. The environment was more natural. There were no computers then and no satellite TV either. For entertainment we had the radio and lots of festivals at local temples. Children today know more about the world around them when they start school. They are also more stubborn and independent than we were. I think these are good characteristics for future citizens in Thailand's modern democracy. I love my work because if I help my students do well in school I know they will have many good career choices and a prosperous future.'

# Landscape and Climate

### North and north-east

The north of Thailand is a mountainous region bordered by Myanmar and the People's Democratic Republic of Lao (Lao PDR). This is the coolest part of the country. Doi Inthanon, the highest point in Thailand, is a popular tourist attraction. Where Lao PDR, Myanmar and Thailand meet is called the Golden Triangle because there is a point from which you can see all three countries. The mountains of the north level out onto the Korat Plateau. This rocky plateau 300 metres above sea-level covers one-third of Thailand.

### Central plains and south

The fertile central plains stretch from the base of the Korat Plateau south to the Gulf of Thailand. Thailand's longest river, the Chao Phraya, flows through these plains providing a year-round supply of water for farming. This area is called Thailand's 'rice bowl' because most of the rice produced in Thailand is grown here.

▼ *Rice fields and a single farmhouse in the fertile central plains of Thailand.*

## IN THEIR OWN WORDS

'My name is Weerachai Nanakorn. I am the Director of the Queen Sirikit Botanic Garden in Chiang Mai Province. Our main job here at the Botanic Garden is to collect and catalogue thousands of plant species, native to Thailand, and to preserve rare and endangered species. An important part of our work is teaching young people to take care of the forests we have left. The forests we have here are part of the last great forests of Asia. Last year we had over 1,000 school groups come to visit from all over Thailand. I like to think we are teaching them to 'grow the forest in their hearts'. Our Botanic Garden is part of a worldwide network. I am very proud of the work we do here because we are preserving Thailand's natural resources for future generations.'

A long, narrow neck of land connects Thailand to Malaysia in the south. Its shores are often battered by fierce storms from the Gulf of Thailand on the east and the Andaman Sea on the west. Large areas of rainforest cover a ridge of hills running the length of the peninsula. Farmers here plant large plantations of pineapples, cashews, coconuts and rubber. Thailand may one day build a canal across this peninsula that would link the Indian Ocean with the South China Sea. In 2003, the government began a study of the cost of building this canal. If the canal is built, it will rank in importance with the Suez Canal linking the Mediterranean Sea with the Red Sea and the Panama Canal linking the Atlantic and Pacific Oceans.

▼ *Islands along Thailand's southern coastlines are home to fishing families, as well as a big attraction to tourists.*

## The monsoons

Thailand has a monsoon climate. Every year, the air moving across the Indian Ocean picks up moisture from the sea. As the moist air blows across Thailand from the south-west, it releases this moisture as rain. The rains usually start in late May or June. It will usually rain heavily at least once every day. Farmers depend on these annual rains to provide water for planting their rice crops. By the end of October, the rainy season is over and the weather gets cooler. The fields are dry and farmers can harvest their rice. By the end of February, the temperature starts to rise again. April (in which the Thai New Year is celebrated according to the Buddhist calendar) is the hottest month of the year. Temperatures average between 30 to 40 °C. Some years there are droughts in parts of Thailand and other years there might be widespread flooding.

## Thailand and global warming

Scientists think global warming might lead to a rise in sea-level caused by melting ice at the North and South Poles. An increase in sea level of 34 to 64 cm over the next 100 years would mean that coastal cities and farmland could be flooded and coastal industries may be lost. Communities in coastal areas may have to be relocated. This would increase pressure on the remaining land and

▲ *A Bangkok river bus navigates in a heavy monsoon storm along the riverbank of the Chao Phraya River in Bangkok. Riverside houses are partly under water due to the rise in sea-level.*

lead to more forest destruction and damage to the ecosystem. Global warming might also change the rainfall patterns. Millions of farmers might not have enough water – or too much water – to grow their crops. Even though these changes are many decades in the future, the Thai government is preparing plans for flood protection and the planning and zoning of activities in coastal areas, including agriculture, industry, transportation and tourism.

▶ *Local market traders are stranded by the floodwaters of Chao Phraya river in Bangkok in 2002.*

## IN THEIR OWN WORDS

'My name is Chavaree Varasai. I'm a climatologist with the Department of Meteorology. My department collects data every three hours from weather stations all over Thailand. We measure things like rainfall, wind speed and humidity to help us predict the weather. Knowing the weather in advance helps farmers and people in industry plan their activities better. Weather changes daily but climate changes are much harder to predict. In Thailand, we have records of weather changes over a period of more than fifty years. Looking at these records we can see that rainfall patterns haven't changed much in the last fifty years but we expect global warming to have some effect on our climate in the future. Already the weather is less predictable from year to year.'

# 4 Natural Resources

## Energy and mineral resources

There are large deposits of coal and natural gas in Thailand and most of its electricity is made by burning oil, coal or natural gas in thermal power plants. Unfortunately, burning coal produces a lot of air pollution. Natural gas supplies about 65 per cent of all Thailand's energy requirements, including fuel for cooking. Oil is used to produce electricity, as raw material for the petrochemical industry and as fuel for cars and trucks. Thailand imports around 80 per cent of the oil it needs.

The government is working hard to promote energy conservation. Thais have used energy from the sun, the wind and from biomass in the past, but mainly for small-scale uses such as pumping water from wells and for drying food. The solar heating industry in Thailand is growing. Over 10,000 square metres of solar heat collectors are installed every year in hospitals, hotels, schools and private homes. Well-managed policies and campaigns on saving energy are making Thais more energy conscious.

▲ *Dams and reservoirs throughout Thailand store water for irrigating farmland and stocking fish.*

◄ *Solar power is sometimes used in rural areas to generate hot water for household use where no other power supply is available.*

## Riches underground

Mines in Thailand produce over 40 minerals. The most abundant are coal, gypsum and tin. Most mining operations use dangerous chemicals that can easily find their way into the food and water supply. Individuals, and groups concerned about the environment, have raised public awareness about the dangers of mining, particularly coal and tin. Their efforts are forcing the mining industry to take better care of the environment.

The most valuable minerals are gemstones. Thailand is famous for its rubies and sapphires. Gemstones and jewellery are one of the country's top ten export industries.

▶ *The Maymo coal mine in the north of Thailand is the largest in Asia, with many more years of coal production available for the nearby power station.*

## IN THEIR OWN WORDS

'My name is Wirat Panomchai. I'm the marketing manager for BPB Thai Gypsum, one of Thailand's largest gypsum products companies. I manage the national sales team for Thailand and our company exports to ASEAN (Association of South-east Asian Nations) countries, mainly Singapore, Malaysia and Vietnam. I like persuading people to use our products because they are environmentally friendly. Gypsum can be used instead of plywood, asbestos sheeting and bricks. That means people are saving forests, reducing health risks and cutting costs when they use our products. Thai gypsum is very high quality so our products have a good reputation. Economies in the region are starting to grow again so my company has great prospects for the future.'

## Agriculture

Thailand is an agricultural country: even though less than 50 per cent of the Thai population earn their living from agriculture. Nearly half of the total land area is used for farming and half of that is used to grow rice. In the past, Thai farmers grew only what they needed for their families and for local markets. In 1961, the First National Economic and Social Development Plan promoted commercial farming. Today Thailand is a leading world exporter of rice, cassava, sugar cane, rubber, orchids and tropical fruits. Large-scale commercial farming needs a lot of land and money for equipment, materials and labour. Big companies can make a profit exporting farm produce to other countries. Small farmers will have to find speciality crops like flowers or medicinal plants or be forced to sell their land. By 2012, the government estimates that less than 40 per cent of the population will be farming.

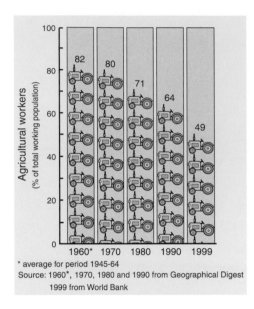

* average for period 1945-64
Source: 1960*, 1970, 1980 and 1990 from Geographical Digest
1999 from World Bank

▲ This graph shows Thailand's strong reliance on agriculture in the past. The number of workers in agriculture has been declining steadily since the 1960s.

◄ In southern Thailand rubber is still an important crop. Tapped from trees the white latex is collected and processed.

## A diminishing resource

The Gulf of Thailand was once a rich fishery. Thai fishermen had easy access to fisheries in the Pacific and Indian Oceans as well. Fish catches have been falling every year for over a decade now.

Since the early 1990s, neighbouring countries have marked off areas of the sea that they control called Exclusive Economic Zones. This is because over-fishing has reduced most stocks of fish to very low levels.

To help make up for the loss, Thailand is promoting fish farming or aquaculture of both ocean and freshwater fish and shrimps. Thailand is now one of the world's largest exporters of shrimp. Producing fish from aquaculture reduces pressure on natural fish stocks, and provides food for people to eat and an income for small farmers and fishermen.

▲ *Fishing boats in port in Songkhla, southern Thailand. Deep-water trawling is still an important industry. Most of the catch is sold for export.*

## IN THEIR OWN WORDS

'My name is Pit Jumpa. That's me in the white T-shirt. I have fished on this lake since I was a boy. Every night my wife and I take our boat out on the lake. We usually wait until after 9 p.m. when the water is calm. We use battery-powered lights to attract the crabs and fish we want to catch. We come back to shore around 5 a.m. and sell our catch at the market. Crabs are selling for about £2 a kilo these days. It's not easy to make a living as a fisherman now. Too many people fish on the lake and every year the number of fish we catch goes down. Our daughter is four years old. We want her to get a good education so she doesn't have to catch fish when she grows up.'

# The Changing Environment

## Shrinking forests, growing cities

Most of Thailand was once covered in thick rainforests. Giant teak trees a metre in diameter were common. Nearly three-quarters of all the forests have been cut down since the 1960s for timber and to make room for new farmland. Cutting the forests destroys the watershed areas of many large rivers. Without the forest cover, the rain washes away the soil that absorbs and holds water for many months. Flooding and soil erosion are now major problems in many parts of Thailand. Loss of forest cover also means that wild birds and animals lose their habitat. Thailand's wild elephant population has fallen to small herds in national parks and there are very few wild tigers left.

## Community forests

There has been a lot of argument between people in communities and the government about the best way to protect and restore the forests in Thailand. The government tried to set up national parks, wildlife preserves and protected

▲ *Much of Thailand's forest has been cleared for new farmland to grow commercial crops such as sugar cane.*

◄ *Sub-tropical forested hills can still be found in the north of Thailand.*

# IN THEIR OWN WORDS

'My name is Sayai Awataw. I am 43 years old. Our family lives in a small village on the south coast of Thailand. When I was a girl, the village was a happy place. There were so many more people and everyone had what they needed to live. The mangrove forests along the shore came right up to the village. The forest provided almost everything we needed. We could catch the fish and crabs that lived among the roots of the trees. We made medicine from the bark and leaves and charcoal from the wood. Most of the mangrove forest is gone now. It was cleared to make commercial shrimp farms. Many people think this was a mistake. Many people in my village are working with a local organization to bring back the mangrove. When I am an old woman I want to go fishing for crabs again.'

forests, but they were not very successful. The boundaries for forest reserves were put up without talking to the local communities. But many people still depend on nearby forests for food, building materials and medicine. In the early 1990s, communities started to put pressure on the government for a national Community Forestry Act. A Community Forestry Act would give local people the right to become involved in the management of local forest resources. They believe the government can depend on them to help protect and restore the forests.

▲ *A sign for a forest reserve close to the Mekong River in north-eastern Thailand. Attempts are being made to rehabilitate small parts of Thailand's remaining forests, but most have disappeared.*

## Urbanization

Approximately 80 per cent of the population live in small towns and villages. Most of Thailand's 73 provincial capitals have less than 100,000 people in each. Bangkok is by far the largest city in Thailand and one of the largest in Asia. It has a population of over seven million people and spills over into neighbouring provinces. Chiang Mai is the second largest city. Pattaya and Phuket have grown from small fishing villages to international resort cities. The eastern coastal area along the Gulf of Thailand from Bangkok to Rayong has become a centre of industry. Thais are quickly learning that not all the consequences of rapid urban development are positive. Most major cities have problems with air pollution and solid waste. Bangkok is the most polluted city in Thailand. Concern for the environment is growing, especially among young Thais.

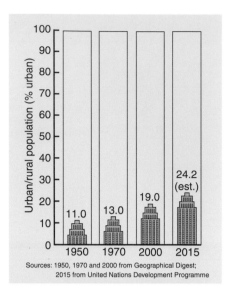

Sources: 1950, 1970 and 2000 from Geographical Digest;
2015 from United Nations Development Programme

▲ *The number of people living in urban areas nearly doubled from 1950 to 2000.*

▲ *A row of newly built homes on the outskirts of Udon Thani, in north-eastern Thailand. Thailand's urban population is growing and demand for houses is increasing.*

# IN THEIR OWN WORDS

'My name is Samart Nasawuan. I am 12 years old. I go to school in the provincial capital. My mother says the schools in town are better. There are lots of interesting things to do and it's more exciting than the village where I live. I like living in the village too but there isn't much work there, so I guess one day I will have to move to the town. I think if we can keep the town environment in good condition, it will be all right to live here.'

## Air pollution

One of the biggest problems in Bangkok is air pollution. Most of the pollution comes from cars and motorcycles. Bangkok streets are narrow and there are daily traffic jams that can last for hours. Tall buildings prevent the wind from blowing the exhaust fumes away. In 1998, the government paid 35 billion baht (£ 0.5 billion) in medical expenses for officials suffering due to dust and air pollution. The situation is slowly improving now that Bangkok has an elevated train system that runs on electricity. The police are more strict about stopping cars and motorcycles that emit too much exhaust.

▼ *The Bangkok skytrain weaves its way through office towers high above city streets, which helps to lessen pollution.*

## A wealth of water

The annual monsoon rains have always provided more than enough water to fill Thailand's lakes and rivers. Over thousands of years, a whole culture of traditions and beliefs has grown up around this annual cycle of rainy and dry seasons. But Thailand's population is increasing and demand for water is growing. Dams and reservoirs built in the 1970s store water that can be used for irrigating farms during the dry season, for raising fish and for recreation. Quantity of water is not a problem but quality of water is becoming a widespread concern. Factory waste is polluting many rivers and small streams. Domestic waste from big cities is also adding to the problem. Chemical fertilizers used in agriculture are being washed into rivers and streams.

▲ *The Loi Kratong festival in late November celebrates the abundance of water at this time of year. These people are carrying Loi Kratong floats to the riverside in Bangkok.*

◄ *Young rice seedlings transplanted into water-filled paddy fields. Thailand is the world's largest rice exporter.*

Thais will have to work hard in the coming decades to preserve and protect their wealth of water. The government has created a National Water Quality Restoration Plan to clean up Thailand's rivers and streams. Part of this plan includes building modern wastewater treatment plants for large cities and industrial areas. There are already 26 treatment plants in operation and 40 more are planned. There are four treatment plants in Bangkok. Large central wastewater treatment plants are expensive and people are not always happy about having one in their neighbourhood. Scientists are finding ways to reduce water waste by inventing processes that use less water, and by recycling. Everyone will have to take some responsibility for using water carefully.

▲ *Farmers in most parts of Thailand have enough water to grow at least one crop of vegetables during the dry season.*

## IN THEIR OWN WORDS

'My name is Pongpob Kanabkaew. I'm 22 years old. That's me in the middle with some of my classmates. All of us are studying for a master's degree in Environmental Education at Prince of Songkhla University. This is my first year. When I graduate, I want to teach people to take better care of our environment. Thailand has developed so fast since I was born. We have a strong economy now but if we damage our environment much more it will be difficult for a lot of people to earn a living. Global warming could be a serious problem for us too. We need to think about this so we can be prepared. I think most people my age want to enjoy a modern life but we also want to protect our natural environment.'

# 6 The Changing Population

### Population growth

In 1900, Thailand's population was eight million people. Today it is just over 60 million. The steady increase in population has been mainly from the birth rate. The average age is 30 years and more than half the population is under 40 years of age. But Thais are having smaller families now and the population growth rate has fallen to 1 per cent per annum, one of the lowest in Asia.

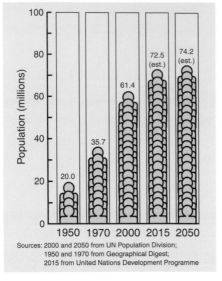

Sources: 2000 and 2050 from UN Population Division;
1950 and 1970 from Geographical Digest;
2015 from United Nations Development Programme

▲ *Thailand's population has increased rapidly since 1950. Its growth is expected to continue, although at a more steady rate in the future.*

◀ *These people are boarding a river taxi. River taxis are a convenient form of transportation for Bangkok's growing population.*

## Population distribution

The average population density for the whole country is 125 people per square kilometre, compared to 238 in the UK. The majority of the population, 80 per cent, live in the countryside, in small villages. This is changing as more people move to towns and cities to look for work and a high standard of living.

## Life expectancy

Thanks to an excellent health care system and a healthy lifestyle, the average life expectancy is 72 years of age for men and 75 for women. This is higher than most other Asian countries. Immunization programmes have reduced infant mortality from 84 per 1,000 in 1969 to 26 per 1,000 in 1996, also a low figure for this region. The biggest health threats to Thais in modern times are similar to those in developed countries, such as heart disease, diabetes, cancer, occupational diseases and mental health problems. HIV-AIDS started spreading quickly in the 1980s. Thailand responded with a highly successful public awareness and prevention campaign that has reduced the infection rate to one of the lowest in Asia.

▲ Families enjoy having picnics and flying kites in their local park. Life expectancy in Thailand is very good. This is helped by having a relaxing lifestyle.

## IN THEIR OWN WORDS

'My name is Mayuree Phongern. I am the Head Nurse of the Family Planning Section at Udon Thani hospital. A large part of my job is counselling families about family planning and birth control methods. I also teach student nurses. I enjoy my work because I am helping families plan a better future. Thailand started family planning programmes about 30 years ago. Today we have one of the lowest birth rates in Asia. In my mother's generation, families of five or six or more were common. Most people today plan to have only one or two children, as people have been taught that it is easier to provide more for their family by having fewer children.'

## Living in harmony

Thai people from many ethnic backgrounds have a reputation for being friendly, hospitable and cheerful. Thailand is sometimes called the Land of Smiles. This is because in Thai culture, a high value is placed on showing respect and getting along with other people. It is very bad manners to get angry or shout at someone and Thai people will work hard to avoid arguments. Children learn to respect their elders and take responsibility for their younger brothers and sisters.

## Indian influence

People from India have been migrating to this region since the first century. Many Thai customs can be traced back to India. The grammar and vocabulary of the Thai language are based on Sanskrit, an ancient

▲ Mosques can be seen throughout southern Thailand. Muslim communities are well integrated into everyday Thai life.

# IN THEIR OWN WORDS

'My name is Nootjaree Sangnoppart. I am 12 years old. This is my cousin, Rutitkarn. He's the same age as me. His other name is Barzilan. That's his Muslim name. My family are Buddhists and his family are Muslims and we all live together. It doesn't seem to matter at all. Lots of people in the south of Thailand are Muslims. Our little town seems to be growing all the time. I hope we get a shopping mall with a good theatre so we can see the latest films. Barzilan wants to be a religious leader when he leaves school. I want to be a civil engineer and travel around the world. I'm very good at maths in school. I also love sport, so I could be a professional athlete one day. Either way, I'm going to go to university for sure.'

Indian language. Indian Brahmins introduced Buddhism to Thailand over 2,000 years ago. Today, Thailand has strong business links with India and many Indian people have settled in Thailand.

Large numbers of Chinese immigrated to Thailand in the early twentieth century, mainly to Bangkok and central Thailand. Along with their business skills they brought their customs, medicine and cuisine. The Chinese quickly integrated into Thai culture. Many Thais, especially in large cities, have Chinese grandparents and China is one of Thailand's top trading partners.

Marriage between Thais and people from other cultures is quite common and widely accepted.

▼ *Buddhism is a part of daily life in Thailand. People often stop at outdoor shrines to offer a prayer.*

### Ethnic hilltribes

Hundreds of years ago, groups of people migrated from the southern part of China into Lao PDR, Myanmar (Burma), Vietnam and Thailand. Living in mountainous and remote areas, their customs and way of life have changed little over time. Today these people are known as 'ethnic hilltribes'.

The major groups living in Thailand are the Karen, Hmong, Yao, Llisu, Lahu, Lawa and Akha. Most tribes live in the mountains in the north and along the border with Myanmar. Each tribe has a distinct origin, language, culture and way of life. In the past, they lived by hunting, trading and growing a few basic crops on mountain hillsides.

### Illegal trade

In the early part of the twentieth century, many hilltribes earned money by growing opium. Now the opium trade is illegal, as is the old practice of burning large patches of forest to clear farmland.

Many hilltribes are finding it difficult to adapt to modern ways. The Thai government is helping hilltribe people develop local industries and encourage tourism. Hilltribe people are now growing crops like vegetables, nuts and flowers for export to domestic and foreign markets.

▼ *Minority groups in the north of Thailand wear distinctive colourful clothing. Young people generally wear modern Western clothing.*

## Preserving tradition

Visiting hilltribe villages is popular with tourists. Hilltribe people usually wear colourful costumes and have interesting customs. Tour companies will take visitors on long hikes or treks into the mountains to visit their villages.

Some people think tourism may be one way for the hilltribes to preserve their traditions and live in the modern world. Others argue that too many tourists will change their culture and damage the local environment.

▶ *Two hilltribe girls take a break from entertaining tourists. Tourism is bringing much needed money into local communities.*

## IN THEIR OWN WORDS

'My name is Nuanchan Pota. I am 66 years old. Until I retired I was a supervisor with the Ministry of Education. Now I'm working on a project helping hilltribe people improve their handicraft industry and market their products. For me this is a new career. I enjoy helping the hilltribe people find new ways to earn a living. Thai people have changed a lot in the last ten or twenty years. People are more independent and more materialistic. Young people are moving away from home and our extended family structure is not as strong as it once was. There are good changes too. People are better educated, healthier and have access to more information. Thais still accept people from other countries and religious backgrounds who come to live here. I think that is a good characteristic of Thai people. I hope it will always be that way.'

# Changes at Home

## Family life

In the last fifty years, family life has changed little in small towns and villages. Families still live together with several generations in the same household or in the same family compound. Thai children have a great deal of freedom, but take responsibility for family chores at an early age. After school and in the evenings, boys and girls will gather at the local schoolyard or temple grounds for a game of football or *tak raw*, a traditional Thai sport that is a bit like volleyball. At meal times, the whole family sits down together for a communal meal. Aunts, uncles and cousins often drop by and visit at meal times. Children are usually included in adult activities and discussions.

▲ *A villager walks back to her house from the fields. Many people are leaving villages in rural Thailand to work in larger urban centres.*

▼ *These children live in a rural village but they may decide to live in the city when they are older, where life is much more westernized.*

# IN THEIR OWN WORDS

'My name is Suphanee Muanhawong but everyone calls me by my nickname, 'Noi'. I am 20 years old. I grew up in a small village with my two sisters. My parents are rice farmers but I work with my aunt in this shop. I never expected to be a shopkeeper but I like it. It's a very different life from farming. I plan to learn bookkeeping so I can help my aunt run her business. Last year I was married. My husband and I are going to wait a few years before we have children though. My parents think this is unusual but I tell them this is the modern way.'

## Modern changes

The extended family tradition is still strong in rural Thailand but it is slowly changing. Young people are moving away to work overseas or in big cities and can only come home at weekends or during holidays. Twenty years ago it was not unusual for girls to marry as young as 15 and have a large family. These days, most young people wait until their early twenties to marry and the average family size is one or two children. Television is replacing traditional forms of entertainment like travelling theatre and musical groups.

Family life in Bangkok is even more westernized. Families are smaller and few people can afford the space for extended family living. Usually both parents work and the family may only have time together at the weekend.

▼ *Families in southern Thailand enjoy the weekend break by picnicking beneath casuarina trees along the coast near Krabi.*

## Education

The literacy rate in Thailand is 96 per cent for men and 92 per cent for women, one of the highest in Asia and equal to the literacy rate in the United States (95.5 per cent). Thai children must stay in school for nine years. The quality of education in Thailand is generally very good, but there are some problems. Teachers are highly respected but not very highly paid. The starting salary for a teacher is about 10,000 baht (£185) per month. This is not a lot of money when rent on a house is 3,000 or 4,000 baht per month. Schools in urban areas are usually better equipped with smaller classes and more teachers than schools in the country. There are few schools for children with special needs.

▲ *Students in urban schools often enjoy modern facilities not available in rural schools.*

◄ *In a small rural school in the hills of northern Thailand, children wrap up warmly as there is no heating in the cool winter months.*

# IN THEIR OWN WORDS

'My name is Pongsaton Benjamak but my friends all call me 'Rut'. I am 13 years old. I like to hang out with my friends after school. After school we all do our homework together. Then we do extra studies in English or play sports or computer games. Everyone studies English in school but Songkhla is a small town and we don't get much opportunity to use our English for real. At the weekends we sometimes go to see a movie. I like Thai pop music and I like to watch satellite TV too.'

## The future of learning

The government is working hard to change the system. Under the new Education Act, local schools will have more control over what students learn. For example, schools in the south of Thailand can introduce religious studies for their Islamic students. Families living in remote areas can set up their own schools at home.

Thailand is fast becoming a centre of learning and education in the region. There are nearly 400 international education programmes, which are taught using English. More students of all ages are coming from neighbouring countries for education and training in Thailand. Thai people know that a well-educated population is necessary for a strong democracy and for trade with other countries.

▼ *Studying English language has become ever more popular as Bangkok becomes a centre for international trade.*

## Diet and health

On a typical day for breakfast a Thai student might have a hot bowl of rice porridge with slivers of boiled egg, dried shrimp and pickled onion. Or perhaps just a mug of hot soymilk. For lunch, noodle dishes, or rice with curried seafood, chicken or pork are popular. Dinner will always include rice with at least three or four choices of topping. Thai food is popular in other countries but it is never as hot and spicy as real Thai food. Thais love to combine many different flavours, colours and textures in one dish. A favourite Thai snack is freshly cut slices of green mango dipped in a paste made from fish sauce, crushed chilli peppers and sugar. Outside of Bangkok, western-style pizza and chicken restaurants have to 'localize' dishes with peppers and other Thai ingredients. Western-style fast food is still a luxury for most Thais.

▲ *Thai students choosing snacks at a local food market during a school break.*

▼ *A food stall serving traditional Thai curries and vegetable dishes. Modern fast food outlets and imported goods are starting to change Thai eating habits.*

# IN THEIR OWN WORDS

'My name is Rattana Wannamanomal. I am 42 years old. I work as the Assistant Front Desk Manager of a luxury apartment building in Bangkok. I work six days a week. I get up very early and I don't get home until late. My working life makes it difficult to find time for my family. When I get home at night, I always make dinner for my husband and our children. I like to cook curries and *tom yam* – a very spicy soup with lots of herbs. On my days off, I like to take my children to the market and teach them how to shop for good-quality food. I think it's important they learn how to cook real food so they don't eat from food stalls and supermarkets all the time. Thai people think good food is good health and I believe it.'

## Health provision

The general health of Thai people has improved a great deal in the last fifty years. Local hospitals and schools teach people about basic health care. The government supports a network of village health volunteers who work at the community level to encourage good sanitation and health habits. The most serious health problems in Thailand now are traffic accidents, heart disease, cancer and occupational diseases.

High standards and low costs have created a whole new industry in Thailand called 'medical tourism'. People from developed countries come to Thailand for medical treatment, cosmetic surgery or dental care and recover in luxury health spas.

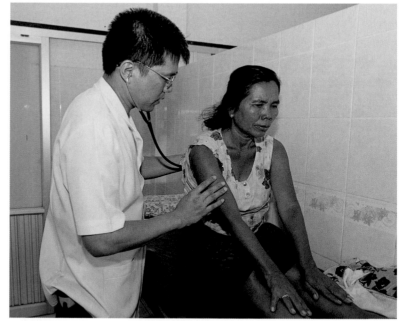

▲ *In a small rural clinic a woman is having a health check-up. Both government and private clinics and hospitals are available, treating patients from all parts of the community.*

## Religion

Buddhism is a part of everyday life in Thailand. More than 90 per cent of Thais are Buddhists. Everywhere you go in Thailand you will see people offering flowers and incense at Buddhist shrines. Early every morning, in every town and village, you will see lines of Buddhist monks, in bright orange robes, making their alms rounds – walking barefoot through the streets collecting their daily food from the people near their *wat*. Thai people believe that the three most important events in a person's life are birth, ordination as a monk, and marriage. In many small villages, the *wat* is still the community centre, school, social welfare agency, rest house and information centre. Monks are expected to set an example for people and to be 'friends, philosophers and guides'. It has been the custom that only men become monks but in recent years, some women have chosen to become monks as well.

▼ *A young man receives a blessing with sacred water and a small mark on the forehead during the yearly festival called Loi Kratong.*

# IN THEIR OWN WORDS

'My name is Sujit Vatanatham. I am 11 years old. I am a novice monk. Every Thai man should be a monk at some time in his life. I will stay here at the *wat* for six months to study Buddhism. There are 20 other boys here with me, but no girls. Every morning we get up at 4.30 a.m. and say prayers for about an hour. Then we go with the older monks on our alms rounds. Alms are gifts of food people give us every day. After breakfast we study Buddhism. We also study regular school subjects. In the afternoon we help the older monks take care of the *wat*. I like being a monk, but I will be happy to go back to my family and my regular school. My house isn't far from here but my parents can't visit every day so we talk on the phone.'

## Life of a monk

Anyone over the age of 6 can be a monk. In many villages, boys will be ordained as monks during the school holidays. You can be a monk for as little as a week or for your entire life. Monks wake up before dawn and practise meditation before making their alms rounds. After breakfast, the only meal of the day, they will study, advise people who come to visit, or take care of the chores around the *wat*. In some *wats*, the monks run schools, run hospices for the sick or elderly and help local communities with development projects.

▼ *Monks sit admiring the view from a hilltop temple in north-west Thailand close to Chiang Rai. It is common for young Thai men to become monks for a few weeks or months in their early teens.*

**From rice fields to factory floors**

Thailand started building modern factories to manufacture goods shortly after the Second World War ended in 1945. To encourage foreign investors to come to Thailand, governments improved the national network of roads, railways and ports. Early investors set up factories for consumer products, car assembly, food processing, pharmaceuticals, and textiles and garments. In 1960, manufacturing contributed only 14 per cent to the Gross Domestic Product. By 1999 this had increased to 35 per cent. The growth of manufacturing created hundreds of thousands of jobs for Thai workers. Many young Thais left their villages to work in towns and cities and enjoy a more modern lifestyle.

▼ *Factories and power stations are taking over the rice fields as the economy changes from agriculture to industry.*

**A growing gap**

Most of the new industries are in urban areas, mainly in and around Bangkok and the eastern coast. The average income of people living in rural areas is half or one-third the income of people living in Bangkok and its neighbouring provinces.

This is a problem because more people want to move to the cities but there are not enough jobs or they do not have the skills to do the work. To help create more employment in small towns and villages, the government created the 'One Village One Product' programme. Many communities are now successfully making and selling food products, furniture and handicrafts all over the world. The government is also providing more support to the Small and Medium Enterprise sector (SME). Small and medium-sized companies employ nearly 95 per cent of the non-agricultural work-force in Thailand.

▶ *A modern crafts centre at Bang Pa near Ayutthaya teaches skills that could easily have been forgotten in the rush towards modernization.*

## IN THEIR OWN WORDS

'My name is Monchaiya Khamsee. I am 26 years old. I live in a small village in north-eastern Thailand. My family are rice farmers. During the harvest, everyone is out in the fields working together all day long. It's hard work but we have fun. I like working outdoors but rice farming doesn't make much money. We will be lucky if we make £250 a year on our one crop. After the harvest, most of the men in the village will go to work in the cities to make more money. They may be away for six or seven months of the year. Life in the village has changed a lot even since I was a girl. It is more boring now because everyone wants to go into the big towns. I want to stay here with my family but the future doesn't look bright for small villages like ours.'

### The 1997 financial crisis

The rapid growth in the manufacturing sector was good for the Thai economy. Thailand had above-average growth rates of 8–10 per cent for several years in the late 1980s. Thailand, once a developing country, was officially classified as a Newly Industrialized Country in the late 1980s. Some people were making lots of money. Everyone believed that the economy would go on growing for ever. People became overconfident. Big companies started spending more than they had and borrowing large sums of money from American and European banks. Thai banks were not very careful about lending money to Thai businesses. The banks lent too much money and people were not paying it back fast enough. This caused a sudden fall in the value of the Thai baht in June 1997. So many businesses went bankrupt so quickly that Thai banks were in danger of collapsing. Suddenly, thousands of people were out of work and hundreds of businesses went bankrupt, including many small banks. Thailand had to ask for assistance from the International Monetary Fund to save the economy.

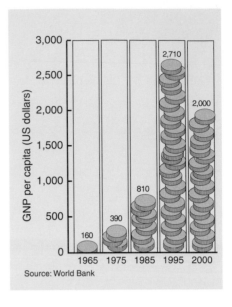

Source: World Bank

▲ *Thailand's GNP soared dramatically from the mid 1980s to the mid 1990s but the impact of the financial crash in 1997 is clearly shown by this graph.*

◄ *The tallest building in Bangkok was built during the financial crash of 1997, and although it was completed later than scheduled, it is a symbol of the regeneration and resilience of the Thai economy. This building is now used as offices for many different businesses.*

## Lessons learned

The crisis ended a decade of steady growth and forced the government to make alterations to the rules and regulations that control the Thai banking and finance sector. The changes were mainly successful and Thailand repaid its debt to the International Monetary Fund in 2002, a year ahead of schedule. Thai businesses became more efficient by introducing international standards for accounting and management. Thai businesses are better managed than before the crisis and many foreign investors are confident that Thailand is now a safer place to do business.

▼ *Business is getting better in Thailand and people's jobs are more secure. These people are travelling to Bangkok to begin their day at work.*

# IN THEIR OWN WORDS

'My name is Bussarakam Chaisuwan. I started working for Capital Nomura Securities as a stockbroker. Now I am a Vice-President in charge of the Individual Services Department. Part of my job is to advise our clients about investments. That means I have to keep up-to-date with world events and local markets. I'm always learning so my job is interesting and exciting. In 1997 our currency, the baht, lost half its value in a short period of time. This caused a big problem for our economy. Many companies, especially finance companies, went bankrupt. A lot of people lost their jobs. Fortunately in Thailand people have an extended family to help out in times of trouble. It was a difficult period but our economy is slowly recovering. I think people in business are better prepared for the future now than before the economic crisis.'

## Tourism

One industry that wasn't affected by the 1997 financial crisis was tourism. Tourism has become one of the most important industries in Thailand. As a tourist destination, Thailand has a lot to offer and Thais are noted for their hospitality. Visitors can trek in mountains and rainforests, or relax on tropical islands with sandy beaches and coral reefs. Resorts such as Pattaya, Phuket and Samui Island are famous throughout the world. Thailand has an ancient culture, delicious food and colourful festivals. In 2001, ten million tourists from all over the world visited Thailand. Tourism brings a lot of money into the country but it can also cause damage to the environment and change local cultures. Water in the Gulf of Thailand is becoming badly polluted as a result of too much tourism. Several years ago, people were advised not to swim in the Gulf and local hotels lost millions of pounds.

▼ *Tourists from all over the world flock to Thailand for holidays. Tourism is one of Thailand's largest income earners.*

A recent trend in the tourism industry is eco-tourism. Instead of sitting on the beach or visiting ancient temples, eco-tourists might go sea canoeing or jungle trekking and learn about local wildlife and village customs. You can go white-water rafting on rivers in the north or cycling on mountain trails. 'Adventure tours' often combine all these activities into a single trip. Thailand wants to continue attracting tourists in large numbers and tourism operators have started to enforce more strict regulations and pay more attention to the environment and local culture.

▶ *Not long ago, this elephant would have been hauling logs out of a forest. Now elephant and* mahoot *(the elephant's handler) earn a good living taking tourists into the hills north of Chiang Mai.*

## IN THEIR OWN WORDS

'My name is Tien. That's it. Only one name. This is my elephant. Her name is Moon and she is 30 years old. Moon and I work together at Mae Sa Elephant Camp near Chiang Mai. We do shows for tourists who come here from all over the world. In my father's time there were still herds of wild elephants in Thailand. Elephants did a lot of work, especially in the forests. Now there is so little forest left and machines have replaced elephants for most kinds of work. The few wild elephants remaining are in national parks. About the only useful work left for elephants now is in tourism. It is very good work looking after elephants. Moon has a better life here than she would in the village. Tourism is helping to preserve elephants in Thailand so I hope people keep coming to see our shows.'

## Marriage customs

In many Asian countries, parents prefer to have sons rather than daughters. Part of the reason is because of marriage customs. In most countries, the family of the bride pays a dowry – a large contribution of money or goods – to the family of the groom. Parents with many daughters can not afford many marriages. In Thailand, parents have always been as happy to have a newborn baby girl as a boy, perhaps because the custom is the opposite: the groom pays a dowry to the family of the bride. Unlike most Asian countries, women in Thailand can select their own marriage partners rather than have a marriage arranged by the family.

## Women at work

Women participate freely in all walks of life and all professions. In some sectors, like manufacturing, commerce and service industries, there are more women working than men. Thai men don't think it unusual to have a woman boss but women in Thailand still experience inequality at work.

▲ *A small boy sits with his grandmother as she weaves traditional cotton cloth on a handloom. Many older people still make craft items that are an important part of the Thai economy.*

◄ *Many women work as teachers in Thailand. Although this is a traditional role, women have a growing reputation for doing well in business.*

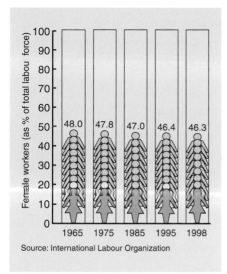

They tend to be paid less for the same work as men. Many professions still favour men for high management positions. Women in Thailand have had the right to vote since 1932 but out of the 500 members in the House of Representatives, only 48 are women. The young women growing up in Thailand today will probably change this. They are better educated and more aware of their opportunities than women in the past.

▲ Almost half of Thailand's workforce are women. This figure has remained constant over the last 30 years.

◄ Young women can choose from a wide range of careers. This woman is germinating orchid seeds in glass jars.

## IN THEIR OWN WORDS

'My name is Piyanut Vorasubin. That's me in the white jacket with my friend Kanlaya. I study civil engineering at the Asian Institute of Technology in Bangkok. I already have a master's degree in engineering in Colorado in the USA. After that I worked as a project manager in the United States for five years. I was in charge of building a department store complex, a hydropower plant and a wastewater treatment plant. Most of the men on my projects didn't mind having a woman for a boss once I proved I was a good engineer. I like engineering because there are always challenging problems to solve. When I finish my studies I plan to work in consulting engineering in Thailand.'

# The Way Ahead

## A choice of possible futures

Thailand has a good climate, a wealth of natural resources and easy access to international trade routes. The people are healthy, well educated and have a democratic government.

Thai people face important challenges in the years ahead. Thai farmers must become more efficient, grow less rice and more high quality export crops if they want to make enough money to continue farming. Industry has to invest more money in training, education and research. The government must learn the lessons of the financial crisis in 1997 and continue to improve business standards and reduce corruption.

Thailand's environment suffered badly during the period of rapid growth in the 1980s. Thai people are becoming more aware of how important it is to manage their natural resources, especially their forests and water. The government must continue to take steps to repair the damage with better legislation and more strict enforcement.

Rapid economic growth has created new problems for Thai society. People are becoming more interested in material wealth. Government policies need to ensure a better distribution of this wealth. People in urban centres earn much

▼ *A buffalo cart and a car share the same stretch of road in the countryside. One of the challenges for Thailand in the future is to narrow the gap between rural and urban living standards.*

# IN THEIR OWN WORDS

'My name is Suphat Khamsee. I'm 18 years old. I am taking my first year of law at Ramkhamhaeng University in Bangkok. I grew up in a small village in north-eastern Thailand. My family are rice farmers. I'm the first person in my family to go to university. Living in Bangkok is a big change for me. There are lots of things to do but it is difficult and expensive to travel around the city. I prefer living in the country. Thailand is a newly developed country and we have a new constitution so law is becoming a more important profession than in the past. I don't know yet exactly what kind of law I want to specialize in but I'm looking forward to the future.'

more money and enjoy a higher standard of living than people in the countryside. A better balance needs to be achieved.

Traditional family values are slowly changing and they need to adapt to modern times without changing so fast that family and social ties break down.

Thai people have a history of successfully keeping up with changes in the world around them. It is very likely they will continue to keep pace with the demands of the twenty-first century.

▶ *Traditional Buddhist architecture will always be a part of Bangkok's skyline, Thailand's future will be a balance of old and new.*

# Glossary

**Alms rounds** Buddhist monks collect offerings or 'alms', usually of food, by making daily 'rounds' or visits in the villages near their temple or *wat*.

**Aquaculture** Raising fish in natural or specially made ponds or in cages in lakes or rivers.

**ASEAN** Association of South-east Asian Nations. An association for mainly economic cooperation between Brunei Darussalam, Cambodia, Indonesia, Lao PDR, Malaysia, Myanmar, Philippines, Singapore, Thailand and Vietnam.

**Biomass** Plant material such as sawdust, tree trimmings, straw, grass, and poultry litter and other animal wastes used to produce energy either by burning or through some chemical reaction.

**Brahmin** A member of the highest Hindu caste (class).

**Buddhist calendar** A calendar based on the death of the founder of Buddhism, Siddhartha Gautama (563-ca. 483 B.C.), also known as Buddha.

**Chedi** A bell-shaped structure used to contain the relics (usually bones) of kings or famous monks.

**Constitutional monarchy** A form of government in which a king or queen is officially the head of state but laws are made by a group of democratically elected officials.

**Consulting engineering** Working as an engineer on short contracts for larger engineering companies.

**Deep-water trawling** Fishing in ocean waters at depths below 15 metres by dragging a large bag-like net behind a ship.

**Democratic society** A political system in which people freely elect a representative government that upholds the rule of law and the rights of individual citizens.

**Exclusive Economic Zone** An area of ocean near the coast of a country over which that country claims the right to control the resources in the sea and on the seafloor.

**Fishery** An industry based on fishing, usually for one or more kinds of fish in a particular area.

**Global warming** The potential increase in the temperature of the earth's atmosphere caused by pollution.

**Green technology** Any product, service or process using renewable materials and energy sources to reduce the use of natural resources and cut down harmful emissions and waste.

**Gypsum** A soft mineral used to make plaster of Paris, fertilizers and building materials.

**Hospice** A centre that provides a home and basic medical care, usually for terminally ill or elderly people with no family.

**Irrigation** Bringing water to farmland using canals and ditches to raise crops in dry areas where there is little water or rainfall.

**Monsoon climate** A climate in which the weather is determined by seasonal wind patterns that bring moist or dry air during certain months.

**Newly Industrialized Country** A country previously classified as a Less Developed Country, but which is rapidly industrializing.

**Opium** A reddish brown gum that comes from poppy flowers and can used to make heroin or medicine.

**Ordination** A religious ceremony in which a man or woman becomes a monk or priest.

**Peninsula** An area of land almost totally surrounded by water.

**Petrochemical industries** Industries that use raw crude oil to produce fuel, plastics and chemicals.

**Plateau** An area of land that is higher than the surrounding area.

**Small and Medium Enterprise** Businesses that employ between 100–10,000 people.

**Solid waste management** Collecting and disposing of rubbish in a way that does not damage the environment or cause health problems.

**Wat** A Buddhist temple in Thailand.

**Watershed** All the land area from which water flows into a river.

# Further Information

**Books for older readers**

*Bridge on the River Kwai* by Pierre Boulle (Asia Books, Bangkok, Hong Kong)

*Khun Tongdaeng: How a common dog won a royal heart* by His Majesty King Bumibol Adulyadej (The Nation Multimedia Group, Bangkok)

*Thai Ways* by Denis Segaller (Post Publishing, Bangkok)

**Useful Addresses**

Tourism Authority of Thailand
4 Ratchadamnoen Nok Avenue
Bangkok 10100 Thailand
Tel: + (66) 22829773
Fax: + (66) 22829775

Thai International Airways
Building 9, 1st Floor, Head office
89 Vibhavadi-Rangsit Road, Bangkok 10900
Tel: + (662) 545-3321
Fax: + (662) 545-3322
E-mail: public.info@thaiairways.co.th

British Embassy
1031 Wireless Road
Lumpini Pathumwan
Bangkok10330 Thailand
Tel: + 66 (0) 2305 8333
Fax: + 66 (0) 2255 8619

**Places to visit**

The Golden Triangle
Chiang Mai Province

Ban Chiang World Heritage Archaeological Site

Crocodile Farm
Samut Prakan Province

Ancient City Theme Park
Samut Prakan Province

Khao Yai National Park
Pakchong, Nakorn Ratchasima Province

Kanchanaburi (site of the Bridge on the River Kwai)

Phuket Island (famous holiday destination)

# Index